Everything Must Praise

Copyright © 2018 by Dr. Galen Gomes Sr., Ed.D.. All rights reserved.

No rights claimed for public domain material, all rights reserved. No parts of this publication may be reproduced, stored in any retrieval system, or transmitted in any form or by any means, electronic, mechanical, recording, or otherwise, without the prior written permission of the author. Violations may be subject to civil or criminal penalties.

ISBN:
978-1-63308-465-0 (paperback)
978-1-63308-466-7 (ebook)

Interior Design by *R'tor John D. Maghuyop*
Illustrated by *James Jordan*

CHALFANT ECKERT
PUBLISHING

1028 S Bishop Avenue, Dept. 178
Rolla, MO 65401

Printed in United States of America

Dr. Galen Gomes Sr., Ed.D.
Illustrated by James Jordan

To my Princes: Galen Jr. and Audwin; and my Princesses: Isabella and Sophia. You all are my inspiration and drive. Know that Daddy loves you and God loves you best of all! No matter who or what we are, we must praise Him. G.G,

To my beloved team that keeps inspiring me to be the best that I can be in everything that I do: Brooke (my awesome Co-Captain), Sydni, Brenden and Skylar. You all are the light of my life. Continue to shine your light! J.J.

This Book Belongs To:

_____

A Child of God

We are all God's children, and as His children, we must honor our Heavenly Father. Although you are just a child, you must understand that God enjoys hearing your praise.

The Bible says that every living thing is required to give God praise.

Psalm 150:6 tells us:

Let everything that has breath praise the Lord. Praise the Lord.

So even as little children, we must learn that no matter who or what we are,

We Must Praise!

Every morning when the flowers bloom,
they're not just trying to take up room.
They raise their heads towards the sky
and open their petals for The Lord on High.

Because …

Everything Must Praise!

Listen closely and you might hear
a happy tune filled with cheer.

When they work,
a great buzz they make,
but the sound is not just for them,
its praise for Christ's sake,

Because ...

Everything Must Praise!

Their very transformation is a testament;
never forget the purpose for which you were sent.
The butterflies give reverence to the One True King
with every flap and flutter of their wings.

Because …

Everything Must Praise!

From the moment they open their eyes,
the birds sing a heavenly lullaby.
They lift their voices and greet the sun,
then sing their praise to the Most Holy One.

Because …

Everything Must Praise!

While Momma watches over with a keen eye,
their fun they will not be denied.
But as the ducklings swim and splash about,
they are singing praises with chirps from their mouths.

Because …

Everything Must Praise!

Playful and seemingly carefree,
everyone in the flock knows their duty.
When the lambs say, "Baa" and prance about,
they're actually doing a praise dance and shout.

Because …

Everything Must Praise!

None prouder: It walks with a sense of royalty,
strutting about as if saying, "Look at me!"
But the peacock spreads his feathers and bows his head,
knowing the most royal of all has commanded and said

Everything Must Praise!

The biggest bird and faster than you might think:
When you hear the ostrich squawk,
it's not random;
with God, it's having a talk.

Because …

Everything Must Praise!

They were given the freedom to prance about,
but the deer give thanks - have no doubt.
So, when they stomp their feet to the ground,
they are hoping to make a heaven-worthy sound.

Because …

Everything Must Praise!

Tall and towering with the trees,
the giraffes munch on the sweetest leaves.
God's provision knows no limit. That is why
they lift their heads to the Most High.

Because …

Everything Must Praise!

As big as they are, they know the truth,
and when God commands, they bow and go mute.
But when the elephant blows its trunk with might,
it's sounding a charge for Jesus The Christ.

Because …

Everything Must Praise!

The largest animals on earth live in the seas.
God gave them His vast waters to travel as they please.
When they breach out the ocean, it's a wonderful sight.
But not even the whale's size is a match
for God's awesome might.
And that's why they jump out the water
and land with a smack!
They have a praise built up, and they can't hold it back!

Because …

Everything Must Praise!

Rough seas are no match for His majesty!
Even the ocean's waves show pageantry
when they splash against the rocks to amaze us
making a thunderous beat for God to hear their praises.

Because …

Everything Must Praise!

Dogs are faithful and obedient – even at play
(and we wouldn't want it any other way).
So when your dog barks at the sky,
know that even she is sending thanks On High.

Because …

Everything Must Praise!

Whether you are waking, at play, or at rest,
you must always try and do your best
to make sure at some point each day without fail,
God has received your praise like a personal email.

And when God receives it, He will surely reply
and send down His blessings from On High.

Because now you know that …

Everything Must Praise!

About the Author

Dr. Galen Gomes Sr. was born in Guyana, South America. He is proud son of the respected Reverend George and Vaulda Gomes and brother to six loving siblings. Galen is forever in love with his wife, Ehasuyi Gomes, and proud father of his sons Galen Jr. & Audwin, and his twin daughters Isabella & Sophia. Galen's academic accomplishments include a Bachelor of Arts from the University at Albany, a Master of Education from Boston College, and an Educational Doctorate in Executive Leadership from St. John Fisher College. This work is the first publication from Dr. Gomes.

www.ingramcontent.com/pod-product-compliance
Lightning Source LLC
LaVergne TN
LVHW071028070426
835507LV00002B/65